Get in the Game

THE BASICS

**Citizens of Hope:
Basics of Christian Identity**

978-1-5018-1309-2 *Study Book*

978-1-5018-1310-8 *eBook*

978-1-5018-1311-5 *Leader Guide*

978-1-5018-1312-2 *Leader Guide eBook*

**The Road to Amazing:
Basics of Christian Practice**

978-1-5018-1313-9 *Study Book*

978-1-5018-1314-6 *eBook*

978-1-5018-1315-3 *Leader Guide*

978-1-5018-1316-0 *Leader Guide eBook*

**Get in the Game:
Basics of Christian Service**

978-1-5018-1317-7 *Study Book*

978-1-5018-1318-4 *eBook*

978-1-5018-1319-1 *Leader Guide*

978-1-5018-1320-7 *Leader Guide eBook*

For more information, visit www.AbingdonPress.com.

The BASICS

Get in the
GAME

basics of christian service

Clayton Oliphint
and
Mary Brooke Casad

Abingdon Press
Nashville

Get in the Game
Basics of Christian Service

To all of the congregations we have been a part of,
with gratitude for shaping us as followers of Jesus.
Each of you, laity and clergy, has challenged us to
"get in the game" and "stay in the game."
We are eternally grateful.

CONTENTS

About the Authors

Clayton Oliphint and **Mary Brooke Casad** are siblings who share a passion for discipleship and helping others grow as followers of Jesus Christ. They grew up in four United Methodist congregations in Louisiana and Texas where their father, the late Ben Oliphint, was pastor. Following his election to the episcopacy in 1980, he served the Topeka and Houston areas. Both Clayton and Mary Brooke are married to fellow "preacher's kids" who share their rich heritage of faith and ministry.

Clayton is senior pastor of First United Methodist Church in Richardson, Texas, a church of six thousand members. He received his undergraduate degree from Austin College and a Master of Divinity and Doctor of Ministry from Perkins School of Theology. He and his wife, Lori, are the parents of three children. Beyond his church and local community involvement, he serves on the steering committee of the Office of Christian Unity and Interreligious Relationships of The United Methodist Church and as a director of the Texas Methodist Foundation Board.

Mary Brooke is former Executive Secretary of the Connectional Table of The United Methodist Church. She served as Director of Connectional Ministries in the Dallas area from 1997 to 2007. Currently, she is a trustee and past chair of the Foundation for Evangelism and a director of the Texas Methodist Foundation Board. She has a degree in journalism from Southern Methodist University and is the author of several *Bluebonnet the Armadillo* children's books, written to teach Texas children about their rich local heritage. She and her clergy husband, Vic, have two sons, a daughter-in-law, and three grandchildren. They live in Sulphur Springs, Texas.

Clayton and Mary Brooke are coauthors of The Basics series. Drawing on their rich faith heritage, they write with a warm storytelling approach that resonates and helps make practical connections between faith and action.

INTRODUCTION

Learning the basics is important in every area of life. This is especially true when it comes to our faith. We tend to make faith extremely complicated. While it is complex, with questions that stretch our minds and imagination, when we focus on the basics, some of that complexity begins to break down. When we gain clarity regarding what God would have us do, it helps focus our lives. Little by little, we learn to seek what God would have us do, and then put our faith into action through service.

When I **(Clayton)** was in junior high school, I went out for the football team. I wasn't very big, and was not very good. In other words, as the coach used to say, "He's small, but he's really, really slow!" I enjoyed being on the team but rarely got into the game. However, on one occasion, our team was winning by a large margin. Sometime late in the fourth quarter, the coach called my name and said, "Oliphint, get in there at defensive end."

"But, Coach, I'm a wide receiver," I said.

11

He growled, "Look, do you want to stand here on the sidelines, or do you want to get in the game?"

And so I ran onto the field, perhaps becoming the smallest defensive end in the history of junior high football. But the coach was right—it's a lot more fun to be in the game!

Every follower of Jesus is faced with a moment of decision like that. Do we stay on the sidelines or get in the game? Jesus indicates in the Gospels that he has come that we might have the abundant life and that the best way to find that life is not through getting everything we want, but through learning to love God by serving others. In following Christ, we are challenged to use our gifts to be a blessing to the world God so loves. Many people looking for fulfillment in life do not understand that. They somehow have bought into the notion that the way to be fulfilled in life is to acquire more possessions, make more money, and have everything you want. But Jesus points us in a different direction. For Christians, getting in the game is about daily decisions to live selflessly, opening ourselves for God to use us in service.

Get in the Game is designed to challenge and encourage you to put your faith in action. Together we will explore the basics of

- Loving God and neighbor;
- Striving to get in "the zone"—to be in sync with what God desires, allowing God to transform us into the servants God wants us to be;
- Living out God's will for our lives through living a joy-filled life, a life of prayer, and a life of gratitude for our many blessings; and

- Accepting the challenge to go "all in" in serving God, especially through living a generous life.

Our hope and prayer is that you will find within yourself a desire to go deeper in your relationship with God through Jesus Christ and that growing closer to God will spur you into action. After all, it's a lot more fun and fulfilling getting in the game than it is to stand on the sidelines!

Clayton Oliphint and **Mary Brooke Casad**

HOW TO USE THIS BOOK

Get in the Game is one of three small-group studies in The Basics, a discipleship series that explores the basics of living as a follower of Jesus. Each study may be done separately or as part of a twelve-week course. Some congregations may choose to use one or all three studies in a churchwide study series.

This book is designed for you, the group member. Each week you will read one chapter and then gather with your group for discussion. (A leader guide with session outlines and other helps is available separately.) If desired, you also may use this book as a personal devotion guide. Before reading each chapter, offer a prayer and invite God's presence and wisdom as you seek to serve God and others.

Our approach throughout is to write on a very personal and practical level, speaking with a unified voice, except when sharing our individual stories (these are identified by our names, which appear in bold within parentheses).

Our hope is that as you read you will feel you are a part of the team, ready to "get in the game."

Each chapter begins with a passage of Scripture, followed by several short thematic readings. At the end of the chapter, you will find a Reflect section where you can record your thoughts in response to specific questions. Drawing on sports imagery, you will be guided by the following:

✗ A Disciple's Playbook

A playbook is a notebook with strategies and diagrams, usually used to outline the execution of football plays. For Christians, the playbook is the Bible. This is the place from which all our study and inquiry begins. Each chapter is based on a passage of Scripture, which is printed at the beginning of the chapter. This section at the end of each chapter invites you to reflect further on the Scripture passage.

◎ Game Plan

A game plan refers to a strategy in sports, politics, or business that has been worked out in advance. This section will invite you to reflect on the major points of each section of the chapter and develop your own game plan for growth by recording the teachings and insights that were most significant for you.

⛿ Score

A score refers to the number of points a player or team has earned in a game. This section invites you to share the "winning point" from this chapter. In other words, what was most memorable about the chapter for you? Was it a passage of Scripture, a story, or a statement? This is an opportunity to write down your main take-away from the chapter.

Your responses to these prompts will help you make personal application and prepare you for sharing with your small group.

As you make your way through this book—whether you are reading it as part of a small-group study or as a personal devotion guide—we hope you will find encouragement and inspiration as a member of the team called to serve Jesus by serving others.

CHAPTER 1

FOCUS ON THE BASICS

When the Pharisees heard that he had silenced the Sadducees, they gathered together, and one of them, a lawyer, asked him a question to test him. "Teacher, which commandment in the law is the greatest?" He said to him, "'You shall love the Lord your God with all your heart, and with all your soul, and with all your mind.' This is the greatest and first commandment. And a second is like it: 'You shall love your neighbor as yourself.' On these two commandments hang all the law and the prophets."

(Matthew 22:34-40)

FOCUS ON THE BASICS

If you could imagine God's perfect game plan for our world, what do you think it would look like? Our role as Christians is to play our hardest at our own positions to make that plan happen. By virtue of our baptism, we are called to get off the sidelines and get in the game, becoming a participant in what God is doing in the world.

So what does it mean, in terms of being a Christian, for us to "get in the game"? Living the Christian life can often be frustrating and confusing. There are so many voices, each seemingly shouting louder than the next one, telling us what being a real Christian should be all about. For many of us, the Bible is confusing and further complicates our understanding of faith. Some of us say, "I love God, and I want to serve God, but I'm not sure where to begin!"

(Clayton) When I played college football, we played an early season game in which our team played terribly. We showed up that day, but our heads were not in the game. We all knew that we were capable of playing better, but we made mistakes. Assignments were not carried out. Blocks were missed. Tackles were not made. Passes were dropped. Silly penalties occurred at inopportune times. Though the score was close, we lost a game we should have won.

Practice the next week was not much fun. As we watched the film of the last game, our coach pointed out all of the mistakes we had made. He told us that we were a better football team than the score indicated and that we needed to focus on the basics. "This game is not that hard," he challenged us. "It's about the basics—blocking, tackling, throwing, catching. That's what we're going to do all week."

Did we ever! It was the hardest week of practices ever. Our coaches worked with us on the fundamentals all week long. We blocked, tackled, threw the ball, caught the ball. We worked on basic assignments. We ran the same basic play over and over again until the coach was satisfied we had it right.

I almost felt sorry for the team we played the next Saturday. Almost. By focusing on the basics, we played the most complete game we had played to that point. We did everything we had practiced—blocking and tackling, throwing and catching, playing with discipline that minimized penalties. And that one basic play? We ran it over and over again successfully, leaving the field with an overwhelming victory against a very fine team.

Who are we as Christians? What are the most basic things we need to remember to guide us in our faith? Many of us talk about, preach about, and fuss about things that are nonessential, and sometimes we forget about the basics. So what did Jesus say was the most important, the most basic thing about our faith? How can we, as God's followers, grow into God's likeness and image in order that we may be a part of God's perfect game plan for our world?

Growing in Christ

When you enter into a relationship with Christ, everything changes. Usually this change is not instant or immediate. Rather, it is a process, which grows out of a relationship. Like all relationships, gradually and over time, you realize you are becoming closer and closer to one another. It begins when you make the decision to give your life to Christ. You might do this because you realize you are not doing the best job directing your life and you need help. Or it may be because you are at a breaking point, at the bottom of a valley looking up at mountains of problems in front of you. Or perhaps you are drawn to the faith community that bears Christ's name. Maybe it's because of radical hospitality, passionate worship experiences, or the way the faith community is involved in mission and service. Whatever circumstance brought you to Jesus, there is a moment of decision to put your life in Christ's hands. Theologians call this *justifying grace*— being made right with God. Just like justifying a text lines up the text correctly, so God's grace works in our lives, forgiving our sins and placing us in a right relationship with God.

In the New Testament, the writings of Paul often talk about being "in Christ." And in 2 Corinthians 5:17, Paul says: "So if anyone is in Christ, there is a new creation: everything old has passed away; see, everything has become new!" This new creation begins a process. Living in a relationship with God, you take intentional steps day by day. You allow God to forgive you, to shape you, to mold you, and to make you into the best version of yourself. As a follower of Jesus, you are growing in grace.

(Clayton) The pillars in the sanctuary of First United Methodist Church, Richardson, Texas, where I serve are cross-shaped. They were lowered into the sanctuary by a crane, to serve as anchors and to hold the building together. For me, they are symbols of "spiritual red-woods," "spiritual giants" that I've known: people who are strong and anchored in their relationship with Christ. People who have the kind of fortitude not to just stand and hold the church up, but reach into the world and show others that there's something more than just what the world offers.

God is love, and God sent Jesus into the world to offer that love to all. Churches exist to welcome people for Christ, to grow people in Christ, and to serve people with Christ. We invite everyone we can to know this love of God and to grow deeper in their relationship with Christ. When this happens, when people begin to grow into these spiritual redwoods, their lives are forever transformed. They go forward into their communities to address the gap between current reality and God's imagination.

These transformed disciples are transforming the world. Our world desperately needs the church to continue to produce spiritual redwoods, people who have been, and are being, shaped into new creations in Christ.

Jesus Gives Two Commandments

The Bible has so much information and so many commandments, so where do we begin? What are the basics we need to focus on as followers of Christ? There is a famous story about the great football coach Vince Lombardi. After his Green Bay Packer team played a particularly bad game, he addressed his team and said, "We're going to get back to the basics!" Holding up a football he then said, "Gentlemen, this is a football!"[1]

Jesus basically gave his own version of that speech when he encountered a group of Pharisees.

Matthew's Gospel tells the story of Jesus being confronted by the Pharisees. The Pharisees were good people; they were religious people. The Greek word for Pharisee (*Pharisaios*) comes from the Aramaic term *peras*, meaning "to divide and separate."[2] These religious leaders separated themselves from the rest of society, in that they were totally dedicated to keeping the law. And in encounter after encounter in the Bible, they were fiercely judgmental of others who, in their eyes, did not keep the law. They were not at all sure about the teachings of Jesus, especially after he turned over the tables in the Temple. Jesus did this because the money changers were cheating people in their exchange of money.

So the Pharisees sought to trick Jesus with a question that would put him at odds with the law of Moses. They asked Jesus: "What is the most important commandment?" That is a great question, especially given the fact that there are 613 commandments in the Torah, the law of Moses, which is given in the first five books of the Bible.[3] That's right—613! The Pharisees dedicated their lives to knowing these laws and living them out. They wrote commentaries about them and debated them constantly, always trying to figure out how they could live them in a way that would honor God.

It is interesting to note that, of the 613 laws, 248 are "positive" commandments and 365 are "negative" commandments.[4] The 248 positive commandments are those like "Remember the sabbath day, and keep it holy" or "Honor your father and your mother" (Exodus 20:8, 12). The number 248 was believed to be the number of bones and major organs in the male body. The 365 negative commandments are those like "You shall not murder" or "You shall not commit adultery" (Exodus 20:13-14). The number 365 is the number of days in a solar year.[5] So if you put that all together, the idea was that, in order to live the law, you would follow God 365 days a year with all of your being. It is beautiful in concept, but trying to remember all 613 laws and live them out steadfastly and fanatically could also be paralyzing. How do you prioritize among all these laws?

So which of the 613 laws is the greatest? Jesus answered their question this way: "'You shall love the Lord your God with all your heart, and with all your soul, and with all your mind.' This is the greatest and first commandment. And a second is like it: 'You shall love your neighbor as yourself'" (Matthew 22:37-39). All of the 613 laws hang on these two.

It was as if Jesus said to the Pharisees, "Gentlemen, this is a football!" Love God. Love your neighbor as yourself.

Love God

So how do we love God with everything we have? If this is one of the most important commandments we can follow, what are practical steps we can take to grow closer to God in this way? What does it mean to give God your heart and your soul and your mind?

There are practical things we can do to intentionally grow closer to God. Through the centuries Christians have found that there are classic disciplines that help us not only stay close to God, but also grow even closer to God. Worshiping God in public and in private has a powerful impact in our lives over time. Studying the Bible—on your own, in a Sunday school class, or a small group—broadens our understanding of who God is and what God desires of us. Holy Communion on a regular basis helps center us in God's grace. Praying alone and with others opens us up to a conversation with God. Fasting, whether it is in the traditional sense of going without food for a meal or a day, or in a different way, such as fasting from social media or television, has a way of creating space and helping us focus on what we really desire—an intimate relationship with God. Generosity, with our talents and our time, gives us special joy as we focus outside of ourselves on the needs of others. Some of these practices may seem obvious to people who are active in their faith, but they are tried and true. There are, of course, many other ways we can experience God, but focusing on the basics on a consistent, ongoing basis can deepen that experience and our awareness of God's presence in our lives. They are the basics of staying in love with God, and they all involve an intentional focus on the part of the believer.

(Clayton) On April Fools' Day, 1989, I went on a blind date. I did not want to go. But I knew that my sister, Mary Brooke, and her friend, who were trying to be matchmakers, would keep pestering me, and so I said, "Okay, let's get this over with." My blind date was a girl named Lori, and I came home from that first date with a pounding heart. I wanted to know more about her. I said to myself that I had to call her and ask her out again. So the next day I picked up the phone and called her and got her answering machine. I called her back again later and spoke with her.

"I had a great time and sure would like to see you again," I said, and proposed another date.

"Oh, I'm so sorry," she said. "I have plans."

I threw out another date about two weeks later, but she had plans for that day too. I had a three-strike rule in those days, and it looked as though I was about to strike out. I proposed another date even further out.

"Oh, I'm so sorry," she said. "I have plans...but I'll change them."

Okay, we'll see where this goes, I thought.

One year later we were married. On the day we got married, I remember thinking, There's no way I could ever love someone as much as I love her right now. There's no way I could ever know someone who knows me for who I am the way she does right now. After knowing each other for only one year, I thought we knew everything about each other.

Twenty-five years later, I look back at that couple who got married after one year of knowing each other and realize that we really didn't know a lot about each other at all. We had the foundation of a relationship, a foundation of love. Looking back over twenty-five years and seeing the ways that our relationship has grown and developed, though, I realize it is more alive today than it has ever been. We have been intentional about spending time together and sharing our life and faith together. The result is a deepening of our love and understanding across the years. I just never imagined that it could ever be better than it was on that first day!

Similarly, our relationship with God and our love for God grows as we spend time with God. There are no substitutes or shortcuts.

In his book *Five Practices of Fruitful Congregations*, Robert Schnase lifts up intentional faith development as one of the practices that results in a deepening spiritual life.[6] This is true for individuals and for faith communities. We've both been in group settings where Robert Schnase has asked this question: "If every member of the church were as intentional about faith development as you are, would this church be growing deeper or dying?" That's a powerful question.

We've heard people say, "Thirty years ago, I accepted Jesus in my heart," and when you ask how that relationship has grown in those thirty years, sometimes they have no response, because too often they have relied on the initial experience to carry them across the years. But can any relationship be sustained without intentionally putting yourself in position to keep it growing? What happened thirty years ago is great, but what's happened in the meantime? Are you growing in your relationship with God? Are you striving after it by intentionally worshiping on a regular basis, not just once in a while, when you feel like it? Are you practicing other spiritual disciplines that will help you grow?

How are we cultivating this relationship of love that God has given us? It is not just a one-time deal where we say yes to God; it is a process where we grow in that love. It is growing closer to Christ, day by day. After saying yes to Jesus in our hearts, we should be able to look back and proclaim: "I'm closer to Christ today than I was thirty years ago." This is the process known as *sanctification*.

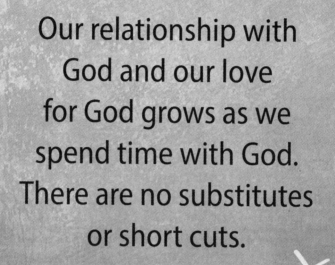

Our relationship with
God and our love
for God grows as we
spend time with God.
There are no substitutes
or short cuts.

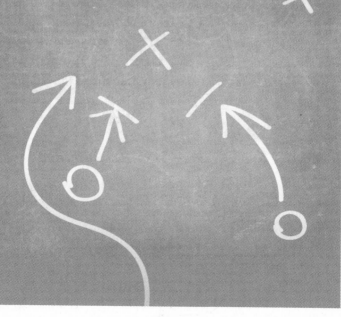

Because we love God, we are invited into a relationship with God that is growing and evolving. God challenges us to live in faith, to put fear behind us, and to move forward in our lives. And here's the more challenging part: as we begin to love God more, how do we put that practice of loving God into the practice of loving our neighbor?

Loving Our Neighbor as We Love Ourselves

Jesus said there was another basic commandment that was as important as the first one: love your neighbor as you love yourself. Now let's be honest: that *is* the challenging part, isn't it? It is so nice to sit in a lovely worship service, in a lovely sanctuary, and say, "Isn't it wonderful to love God? I love God. Don't you love God? I love that we can all love God and worship God together." But we barely make it into the parking lot, into our cars, before we are fighting about who gets out of the parking lot first!

How do we put "loving our neighbor" into practice? That's the challenge of faith. How do we leave the church building and give God's grace and love to others? That takes intentional effort and practice. One of the most practical ways to start doing this is to ask ourselves, what is the current reality in our neighborhood or community? What might be God's imagination for that reality? What can we and other Christians do to close the gap between current reality and the world that God imagines? God so loved the world in general and the people within it specifically. So how can we love people as God would have us love them? We can all find at least one way.

(Clayton) Several years ago some members of our church began a conversation with a nearby public school. One of our members had taught at the school and knew the needs were profound, with more than 90 percent of the children living at or below the poverty level. In talking to the principal of the school, they simply shared a desire to be good neighbors, asking the question, "As neighbors who care, how can we help?" It took a while to allay the fears of the principal that there was a hidden agenda behind the question—there wasn't. We weren't trying to get people to come to our church, save them, or manipulate them in any way. We just wanted to be good neighbors.

Fast forward several years to a true partnership that has been forged between our congregation and the school. The school trusts us because we have built a relationship with it. Our relationship has blessed our church every bit as much as our church has blessed the school. We have worked alongside the teachers and parents of the school in an effort to enhance the educational experience of the children. It is a beautiful thing to see neighbors loving neighbors.

We are called to be loving toward our neighbors, to treat our neighbors as we ourselves would want to be treated. Jesus summed it up: everything in the law, in the 613 laws, is about loving God and loving neighbor. And he had one more thing to say that is often overlooked: "Love God and love neighbor *as you love yourself.*" Many of us struggle to love God and to love our neighbor because we haven't come to terms with our own identity.

Do you know that you are a child of God? Do you know that God looks at you and smiles and delights in who you are? You are a gift. And the way you love yourself often has bearing on how you love those around you: in your homes, in your school, in your neighborhood, in your workplace, and with the strangers you meet. It also has a bearing on how you love God. It's all tied together. God calls us to join together in this struggle of remembering who we are, because it's hard. We are striving to grow in our relationship with God, to understand that God loves us, that God has given Jesus for us. We are striving to love God even more, every day of our lives.

God has blessed us. So how do we return thanks? How do we put this love we've experienced into action? By treating those around us as we would like to be treated ourselves. And how do we begin to love ourselves, to be a little easier and gentler? By trying to remember every morning that we have an opportunity to be in this relationship as a child of God—to love God, to love our neighbors, and to love ourselves.

(Mary Brooke) I remember sitting in church one Sunday morning when the words came to me. (My husband likes to think it was inspired by his preaching—and maybe it was!) I quickly jotted them down on my church bulletin: "To see the Christ in others, to be the Christ for others." I decided the words had come as a gift from God, and they would be my personal mission statement.

Since then, I write this mission statement at the top of my prayer list every morning. It serves as a reminder that every person I will encounter that day is a beloved child of God. Jesus noted in Matthew 25 that when we serve others, it's the same as if we were serving him. "To see the Christ in others" is a recognition that Christ dwells in all creation. It requires me to respect and honor all people, to treat them with kindness, patience, understanding, and love. It compels me to view all of God's creation as holy and sacred.

"To be the Christ for others" is quite challenging! It means that I am striving to reflect the love of Christ in my words and actions. I'm striving to share the good news of the gospel of Jesus Christ. I'm asking myself that popular question: "WWJD?" (What would Jesus do?)

So, as you've probably already surmised, I fail to accomplish my mission on a daily basis! With gratitude for Christ's forgiveness and grace, I simply try again the next day, and the next. But these words give me a quick and memorable focus about my mission each day: "To see the Christ in others, to be the Christ for others."

Get in the Game

So, are you ready to get off the sidelines and into the game? Are you ready to commit today to growing in your relationship with God, with your neighbors, and with yourself? Our challenge is to grow into "spiritual redwoods" that are so steeped in this love of God that we can't help ourselves from reaching out, welcoming others, and serving them in the spirit of Jesus Christ. God has a plan for each of our lives—a vision for whom God created us to be.

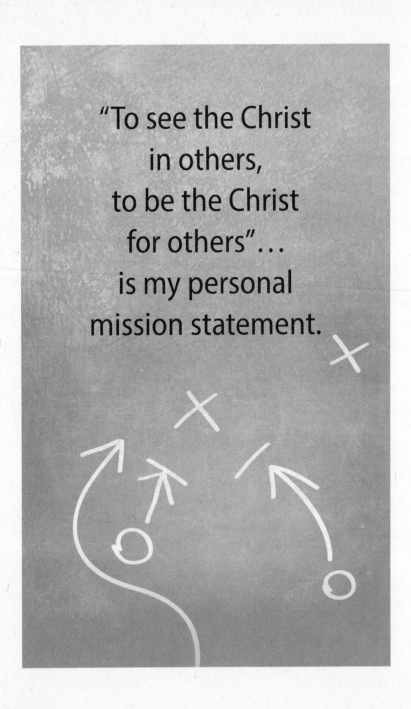

"To see the Christ
in others,
to be the Christ
for others"…
is my personal
mission statement.

It may be time for an honest assessment of our current reality and to recognize the gap between where we are and what God imagines. To become the person God imagines us and created us to be. To become a blessing to others, loving our neighbors as we love ourselves.

Don't be overwhelmed by the enormity of the task. Sometimes we get so caught up in the details that we ignore the basics. Just focus on the basics, loving God and loving your neighbors, and trust God with the rest.

O God, I spend far too much time worried about things that, in the long run, are not that important. Forgive me for majoring in the minors. Help me to focus on the basics today. I love you with everything in my being. I want to serve you. Help me to see you in my neighbor and to truly learn to love my neighbor. Let me judge my neighbors less and love them more. And Lord, help me this day to accept that you love me, and that I can love my neighbor more fully when I learn to love myself. Thank you for the opportunity to get off the sidelines and get in the game today. With everything in my being, I will strive to serve you. In Jesus' name. Amen.

REFLECT

ⅩA Disciple's Playbook

Reread Matthew 22:34-40 (see page 20).

In this Scripture passage, Jesus summarizes the 613 laws of the Torah into one compelling commandment: Love God with everything in your being, and love your neighbor as yourself. Jesus was lifting up two teachings found among the 613.

First, he was referencing what is known as the Shema, one of the most important sayings of the Jewish people: "Hear, O Israel: The LORD is our God, the LORD alone. You shall love the LORD your God with all your heart, and with all your soul, and with all your might" (Deuteronomy 6:4-5). This law is what separated the Hebrew people from other cultures, many of whom were polytheistic—meaning they worshiped many gods. The Jewish people believed fiercely in the ideas that there is but one true God and that God alone is to be worshiped.

The second law Jesus was drawing on was this: "You shall not take vengeance or bear a grudge against any of your people, but you shall love your neighbor as yourself" (Leviticus 19:18). Jesus explained that everything in the law and the prophets hangs on these two sayings. The challenge is translating one's love for God into love for neighbor. Because you love God, you strive to love your neighbor as yourself.

In Luke's version of Jesus' encounter with the lawyer (Luke 10:25-37), the lawyer pushes the issue and asks the question, "And who is my neighbor?" In response, Jesus tells the story of the good Samaritan. What does it mean for us to show compassion for others? How can we make the love we have for God more tangible? What does loving our neighbor look like in action? What does loving myself have to do with loving God and neighbor? All of these questions and more confront us in this great commandment. We are to love God and love neighbor as we love ourselves.

What is the most practical way to show your love for God and neighbor?

◎ Game Plan

What insights did you gain from each section of this chapter?

Growing in Christ

Jesus Gives Two Commandments

Love God

Loving Our Neighbor as We Love Ourselves

Get in the Game

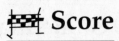 **Score**

What's the "winning point" you will remember from this chapter?

CHAPTER 2

GET IN THE ZONE

I appeal to you therefore, brothers and sisters, by the mercies of God, to present your bodies as a living sacrifice, holy and acceptable to God, which is your spiritual worship. Do not be conformed to this world, but be transformed by the renewing of your minds, so that you may discern what is the will of God—what is good and acceptable and perfect.

For by the grace given to me I say to everyone among you not to think of yourself more highly than you ought to think, but to think with sober judgment, each according to the measure of faith that God has assigned. For as in one body we have many members, and not all the members have the same function, so we, who are many, are one body in Christ, and individually we are members one of another. We have gifts that differ according to the grace given to us: prophecy, in proportion to faith; ministry, in ministering; the teacher, in teaching; the exhorter, in exhortation; the giver, in generosity; the leader, in diligence; the compassionate, in cheerfulness.

(Romans 12:1-8)

CHAPTER 2

GET IN THE ZONE

When playing sports, it's exciting to get off the sidelines and get into the game. But the game can be fast and furious, overwhelming at times, even if you've played the game before. This is true in sports, and it's also true as we strive to live lives of faith. In order to play the game with excellence, we've got to learn the basics of how to play and get a feel for how it all works. And how do we do that?

By practicing, over and over again. Through practice, challenging aspects of the game become almost routine over time, and playing the game becomes second nature. In sports they call this "getting in the zone."

The Zone

Have you ever seen an athlete playing in "the zone"—that moment when everything just comes together? Talent certainly plays a role in those moments, but clarity and focus make the difference. Everyone else seems to be just playing the game, but an athlete in the zone is locked in, totally present in the moment, and has a feel for the game that sets him or her apart. It's like watching Jordan Spieth play an amazing game of golf or Serena Williams dominate a tennis match. Sometimes when an athlete is interviewed after a game, he or she will say something like, "I don't know exactly what happened. I was just in the zone today."

(Clayton) I played wide receiver at a small college, and in my junior year we won a national football championship. About every five years, the team gets together for a reunion, and the quarterback and I always end up reminiscing. Our spouses' eyes will roll as one of us inevitably says, "Do you remember that play in the semifinal game?"

It was in the fourth quarter, third and long. We needed a critical first down, and it was a pass play to me. For some reason, I ran the wrong route. I was on track until I got to the point where I was supposed to break to the sideline, and for some reason I still can't explain to this day, I turned inside. When I turned around, the ball was there. It almost knocked me over, but somehow I managed to hang on for a first down. If the quarterback had thrown the ball to the right spot, and I had run the route the wrong way, it would have been intercepted.

And if I had run the right route and he threw the ball to the inside as he did, it also would have been intercepted. But I ran the wrong route, turned, and the ball was there!

How did that happen? We were in the zone. We were on the same page. It was no accident we were in "the zone" because the real answer was, we had put in the time. Two years earlier, the quarterbacks and receivers had made a decision that we would get to practice early every day. That turned into a thirty-minute ritual, then an hour. After practice, we stayed on for fifteen or twenty minutes, then forty-five minutes or an hour every day after practice.

How do you know it's going to work in a game? Put the time in, over and over and over again. Football seemed like such a fast game to me when I was a freshman. It was scary and wild, and I didn't know what to do. But after years of practice, it all came together in such a way that the game slowed down and allowed me to be present during play.

Being in the zone allows you to slow down and see things more clearly. This can happen, not just in sports, but in our relationships as well. Sometimes there's a synchronicity in our relationships, when everything comes together in such a wonderful way; you are "in sync" with another person. Perhaps it's a colleague, someone you've worked with for some period of time. You get in a zone together. You read each other's thoughts, and are able to pinpoint the right direction for your work. It happens in friendships, as you take time to get to know another person and develop a level of trust and respect. It happens in marriage, when a couple invest time in the relationship, have a shared set of values, and walk hand in hand toward common hopes and dreams. There is something about the investment of time in a relationship. Have you ever witnessed couples who have been married for a long time often finish each other's sentences? The investment of time and love, along with the giving of self, comes together in a beautiful synchronization.

Get in the "God Zone"

What about your relationship with God? Have you ever been in the "God Zone"—a time during which you felt "in sync" with God, striving to do God's will and work, and it came together in such a way that you felt God was pleased with the way you were living your life? If being in the zone makes sense in sports and in our relationships, it can also make sense in our relationship with God. Paul gives us a wonderful outline for living in the God Zone, for living a life in sync with what God would have us do. The first verses of Romans 12 are filled with instruction for us: "I appeal to you therefore, brothers and sisters, by the mercies of God, to present your bodies as a living sacrifice, holy and acceptable to God, which is your spiritual worship" (v. 1). Paul is telling us we have to give ourselves fully to God, invest ourselves fully. Being a Christian is about being "all in" and fully committed.

What is Paul saying to the people? God did not ask them for an animal sacrifice. In the Old Testament we often read about people bringing an animal to sacrifice before the Lord as a way to be forgiven for various sins and transgressions. They understood this sacrifice as a symbolic act of atonement to right themselves with God. Is this the sacrifice God wants from us? Or is it a changed heart, with a life fully committed to God? The prophet Micah said it so well:

> *"With what shall I come before the LORD,*
> *and bow myself before God on high?*
> *Shall I come before him with burnt offerings,*
> *with calves a year old?*
> *Will the LORD be pleased with thousands of rams,*
> *with ten thousands of rivers of oil?*
> *Shall I give my firstborn for my transgression,*
> *the fruit of my body for the sin of my soul?"*
> *He has told you, O mortal, what is good;*
> *and what does the LORD require of you*
> *but to do justice, and to love kindness,*
> *and to walk humbly with your God?*
>
> *(Micah 6:6-8)*

In Romans 5, Paul had clarified that the sacrificial love of Jesus and his love alone can make us right with God. In Romans 6, Paul reminds us of what God has done for us in Jesus: "The death he died, he died to sin, once for all; but the life he lives, he lives to God. So you also must consider yourselves dead to sin and alive to God in Christ Jesus" (Romans 6:10-11). God has already done the heavy lifting through the life, death, and resurrection of his Son, Jesus. What sacrifice does God require of you? A changed heart, a heart fully devoted to living for God.

In order to do this, you are called to surrender. To present your whole self, and to recognize that there is a

God, and it's not you. You are not the Creator, God is. You are not the Shepherd, God is. When you can acknowledge this, you will no longer live for yourself, but for God. Instead of telling God your agenda, you now seek to align your life with God's agenda.

What is our "spiritual worship" (Romans 12:1)? It's how we live our lives. Psalm 100:2 says, "worship the Lord with gladness." This can also be interpreted as "serve the Lord with gladness" (NKJV) or "serve the Lord with celebration" (CEB). Our worship is our service to God, and our service to God is our worship. It is our whole being engaged in living for God, seeking to be on the same page with God in all we do.

Transformed in the God Zone

In Romans 12:2, Paul says, "Do not be conformed to this world, but be transformed by the renewal of your minds, so that you may discern what is the will of God— what is good and acceptable and perfect." What Paul is talking about is an overwhelming and unfortunate reality in our lives: we tend to look more like the world than we look like Christ.

We are easily deceived into being conformed to the ways of the world rather than being transformed by the renewal of our minds. What does it mean for us to be renewed in our minds? It is about letting Christ transform our lives so that our hearts and minds reflect the mind of Christ. It's like what Paul said to the church at Philippi:

Let the same mind be in you that was in Christ Jesus,

> *who, though he was in the form of God,*
> *did not regard equality with God*
> *as something to be exploited,*
> *but emptied himself,*
> *taking the form of a slave,*
> *being born in human likeness.*
> *And being found in human form,*
> *he humbled himself*
> *and became obedient to the point of death—*
> *even death on a cross.*
>
> *(Philippians 2:5-8)*

What would it mean for you to align your thoughts with the thoughts of Christ? Would you show more humility? More compassion? Would you be slower to judge others and quicker to accept others? Would people say about you that you lived more for yourself, or more for others? In what other ways could your life better reflect the life of Christ? Are you being conformed to the world, or is your life being transformed by what God is doing in renewing your mind?

(Mary Brooke) When our son McCrae was eleven years old, he was part of a wonderful confirmation class at our church. Over many weeks of shared study and service experiences, these young people discovered what it means to claim the promises that were made on their behalf at baptism and profess Jesus Christ as Lord and Savior. On Confirmation Sunday, the church was filled with family and friends who came to support and encourage the confirmands.

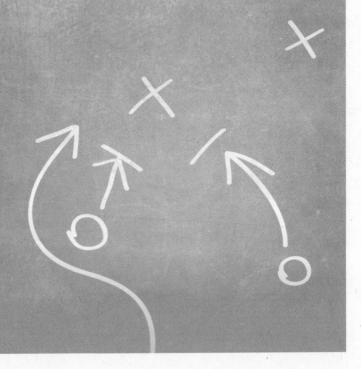

Our worship is
our service to God,
and our service to God
is our worship.

Part of the Confirmation Service was the presentation of a banner created by the confirmation class. The hands of each confirmand were traced and cut out in felt to display on the banner. The design was lovely, but I blinked my eyes several times to make sure I was reading the banner correctly. Instead of "Confirmation Class," the banner read "Conformation Class."

The misspelling of the word *confirmation* made for a great theological conversation over lunch that day. Everyone agreed that their thoughts had gone to the Romans 12 passage of not being "conformed to this world." The confirmands had just made promises to do anything but that, renouncing and rejecting wickedness and evil, repenting of sin, accepting freedom and power from God to resist injustice and oppression, putting their trust in the grace of Jesus and committing to serve him in union with the Church, opened to all people.[1]

It's a daily struggle for most of us to resist being a part of a "conformation" class. We need the body of Christ to remind us of God's promises, which we have claimed and confirmed as our own. We need time in prayer and Bible study to keep us in sync with the leading of the Holy Spirit.

In order to be transformed, we have to open ourselves to transformation. In every situation, we seek to discern God's will for us. This takes a lot of practice. We don't always know what God's will is in every given situation. But there is something about the very act of humbling ourselves before God, praying for God's direction in each circumstance, and then striving to live toward that direction that brings us a different sense about life. As we do this day by day, our lives are being transformed.

God's grace is shaping us and molding us so that we become more Christlike in our spirit and actions. Rather than being conformed to the world around us, we are ready to live in the God Zone.

Living in the God Zone

As we strive to live in the God Zone, there is a qualitative difference in our lives. Maybe this is what Jesus meant when he said, "I came that they may have life, and have it abundantly" (John 10:10b). This abundant life is a life of joy. Some people see Christian faith as a burden or a duty. What God offers us is freedom from burden. When we let go of ourselves and strive to follow God, it is the most freeing experience in the world. Jesus didn't just want us to experience this after we die. This abundant life—this eternal life—is possible here and now.

Are there signs that we are in the God Zone? Certainly there are moments, sometimes fleeting, sometimes steady, when we sense with deep humility that we are on the same page with God. Certainly you might be living in the God Zone if

- You have an overwhelming sense of being blessed.
- You are humbled by what God has done for you in Christ.
- You feel loved and accepted by God—not because you are good.
- You have discovered that your life has meaning and purpose beyond yourself.
- Your heart is broken by the things that break God's heart.

- You have a growing awareness of the disparities in life, and a sense that you are called to be a part of God's answer by seeking justice for all people.
- You are looking for Christ in the face of your neighbors, and even strangers.
- You've ever felt a peace that passes all understanding in the midst of a chaotic situation.
- You are troubled about the treatment of the "least of these" (see Matthew 25:40).
- You experience uncontrollable fits of joy for no reason, other than you are grateful to God for the gift of life itself.

God sent Jesus Christ in the world to show us the way to live in the God Zone in the here and now. God has given us this incredible gift called life. How do we begin to experience that?

(Clayton) Recently my son and I went to a 3-D movie and they gave us 3-D glasses when we walked in. The quality of the picture was amazing, and everyone in the audience flinched several times, as it seemed as though things on the screen were jumping out and about to hit us. About halfway through the movie, I decided to take my glasses off and see what the movie looked like without them. What a difference! Everything on the screen was blurred. There were many images being displayed at once, but they were all separated from one another. It took putting the glasses back on to bring all of the different images together to form one incredibly clear picture.

When we open ourselves to God's transformation, we are putting on the glasses of grace. God's grace gathers the broken pieces of our lives, bringing clarity and purpose. And the picture quality is amazing. We are able to see in ways we never have before how God is a part of everything we are. We have a clearer sense of how all of life works together, and how God is working for good in all things.

God's grace makes all the difference. Our part is to follow and to invest our lives in basic spiritual practices that pay off. As in sports, success comes when we show up and put in the time every day. Slowly but surely, that investment begins to pay off and the game slows down. We gain clarity as we begin to see ourselves as children of God, blessed with a sense of great purpose. God has called us to live the abundant life, and we've been blessed in order to be a blessing to others. We are ready to use our gifts to help heal the world that God so loves.

Serving in the God Zone

Paul continues his instructions to the Romans by encouraging them to use the varied gifts they have been given. In Romans 12:3, he reminds us "not to think of yourself more highly than you ought to think." Paul speaks like a coach addressing a team. Each member is important, but no one player is more important than the team. He's challenging each one to maximize his or her own gifts while being transformed by God's grace. But he also reminds them that they are all a part of the same team—the body of Christ. Each has a role to play in blessing the world by sharing God's love. While the team goal is the same, each member has a unique gift to offer.

The body of Christ functions at its highest level when all strive together to be in the God Zone, honoring one other for their contributions.

Have you ever thought about the gifts you've been given? Are there ways God has equipped you through your talents, through experiences you have had in your life, or through your education (formal or informal) that God can use as a blessing in our world? Having gifts that differ, we are all called to get off the sidelines and get into the game. Every one of us can make a difference. Every one of us is important to the whole. In Romans 12:6–8, Paul gives us examples of varied gifts that exist in the body of Christ: prophecy, ministry, teaching, exhortation, giving, leading, and compassion. The list was not meant to be exhaustive, but was given to stimulate the thinking of the Roman Christian audience. After hearing this message, the question they were probably asking themselves was, *What gift can I offer to the body of Christ?* How would you answer that question?

One of the most beautiful things to witness is the various ways in which members use their God-given talents to bless not only the church, but also the world. Just look at a typical Sunday in a church. Musicians play and sing to the glory of God. Sunday school and small-group leaders prepare and lead discussions and lessons. Some clean in order to prepare the sanctuary and classrooms, and others stay around to clean up after. Ushers open doors, welcome people, pass out bulletins, and collect an offering. Some stick around to count the offering. A pastor or a lay leader delivers a message. Congregation members pray and sing and worship. The body of Christ in action is an amazing thing to behold.

Having gifts that differ,
we are all called to
get off the sidelines
and get into the game.
Every one of us can
make a difference.

But it doesn't stop there. When the worship is over, that's when the real service begins. Or you could say, when the service is over, the worship begins. We go into the world to worship God by serving God. We all have ways we can be a blessing and every gift matters. God has called us to go into our homes, our neighborhoods, our schools, our communities, our nation, and all the world, using the gifts we have been given to offer the hope of God's love.

Beyond what you *do*, in terms of serving your own faith community, how are you offering your gifts to bless the world? This is an important question for every Christian to consider.

(Clayton) A woman in my church was living out her last days in a nursing home, frustrated that her body was failing. Over the years, she had held many positions of responsibility in the church—she had taught and led in ways that had inspired others to serve. Now she was no longer able to come to church and could barely get out of bed to care for her own needs. On one visit she expressed this frustration: "I'm no use to anyone anymore. I just don't know why the Lord is leaving me here. I'm just wasting money and taking up space." We talked and prayed together, and I assured her that she still was needed and wanted, and that her gifts could still be used in ministry.

The next time I saw her, her eyes were lit up with joy. She said, "I've found a way for God to use me!" She told me about her realization that her ministry now was prayer and hospitality. She prayed daily for her pastors. She got our prayer list from the church and prayed for every person listed. Whoever came into her room, she tried to welcome as if Christ had walked into her room. She could rarely get out, but when she did, she tried to speak to others and ask about them. When she died about a year later, all of the staff from the nursing home came to the service, and several testified about how this sweet woman had shown them the love of God. She was living in the God Zone.

Going Forward

Paul's letter to the Romans challenges us in multiple ways: Each of us is called to put our whole selves in, to live sacrificially for God. We allow God to begin the work of transformation in our hearts and minds, refusing to be conformed to the world; and we are called to discover the gifts God has given us, considering how we can use these gifts in ministry to bless the world. All of this is about getting in the zone, and there is nothing like it! There is no gift that would be greater for you to share. There is no sense of purpose or meaning in life that is any greater or more worthy of obtaining. God is calling us to life! May we claim it, live it, and invest in it.

God, I want to live my life in alignment with you. This day I give myself fully to you. Take my life. Let me not be conformed to the world. Begin the work of transforming me into the person you desire me to become. Give me realistic perspective about the gifts you have given me, and help me to use those gifts to be a blessing to the world. I want to serve you as long as I have breath. Let me help someone today. Help me to strive for justice with everyone I meet this day. Let my life reflect your love to others, and help me to stay in the zone of your grace and love. In Jesus' name. Amen.

 **REFLECT**

X A Disciple's Playbook

Reread Romans 12:1-8 (see page 42).

Paul gives us a wonderful outline for living in the God Zone, for living a life in sync with what God would have us do. The first verses of Romans 12 are filled with instruction for us. Paul is telling us we have to give ourselves fully to God, invest ourselves fully. Being a Christian is about being "all in" and fully committed.

What is Paul saying to the people? God did not ask them for an animal sacrifice. In the Old Testament we often read about people bringing an animal to sacrifice before the Lord as a way to be forgiven for various sins and transgressions (see Genesis 4:4-5). They understood this sacrifice as a symbolic act of atonement to right themselves with God. But now, because of what Jesus, the Lamb of God, has done for us on the cross, animal sacrifice is no longer necessary (see Hebrews 7:27). Instead, Paul urges our very lives to become a living sacrifice, to put God's agenda ahead of our own.

Paul then encourages followers of Christ in Romans 12:2 to "not be conformed to this world, but...transformed by the renewing of your minds." Christians are challenged to be distinguishable from the rest of the world, not adopting the values of the world, but staying

59

connected to Christ. Through this connection God does the work of transformation, changing our minds, our thoughts, and our internal conversations to more closely mirror the mind of Christ. This internal conversation shapes our thoughts and actions over time, enabling us to have greater discernment about what God would have us do.

Being more closely aligned with God's will, we are then challenged in Romans 12:3-8 to consider, "with sober judgment," how our gifts can be used in God's mission. We are part of the body of Christ, an image Paul also uses in 1 Corinthians 12. We all have different gifts and should use those gifts as we have been so blessed. The question every Christian must answer is, "What gifts do I have that can best serve the cause of Christ?" It is also critical to remember that every person has gifts and they are not the same. Yet, we all are part of the one body. How can we honor the gifts of each member of the body, as we strive together to do what is pleasing to God?

What sacrifices have you made for God?

What gifts have you used in serving God?

◉ Game Plan

What insights did you gain from each section of this chapter?

The Zone

Get in the "God Zone"

Transformed in the God Zone

Living in the God Zone

Serving in the God Zone

Going Forward

 **Score**

What's the "winning point" you will remember from this chapter?

CHAPTER 3

TRAINING

*Rejoice always, pray without ceasing, give thanks in all
circumstances; for this is the will of God in Christ Jesus
for you.*

(1 Thessalonians 5:16-18)

*On the way to Jerusalem Jesus was going through the
region between Samaria and Galilee. As he entered a
village, ten lepers approached him. Keeping their distance,
they called out, saying, "Jesus, Master, have mercy on
us!" When he saw them, he said to them, "Go and show
yourselves to the priests." And as they went, they were
made clean. Then one of them, when he saw that he was
healed, turned back, praising God with a loud voice. He
prostrated himself at Jesus' feet and thanked him. And he
was a Samaritan. Then Jesus asked, "Were not ten made
clean? But the other nine, where are they? Was none of
them found to return and give praise to God except this
foreigner?" Then he said to him, "Get up and go on your
way; your faith has made you well."*

(Luke 17:11-19)

CHAPTER 3

TRAINING

Every athlete knows that if you are going to play the game at a high level, you have to constantly train to get better. Practicing may not actually make you perfect, but you will find yourself improving, perhaps a little, perhaps a lot, if you will work at it. Training has to do with focusing on the basic things, but it also means stretching yourself. Some things do not come naturally to us, but through regular practice, we can learn to do them and do them well. This is true in sports, and it's true in our walk with God.

(Clayton) When Mary Brooke's eldest son, McCrae, turned one, we had a family birthday gathering. McCrae was the first grandchild on both sides of the family, so his birthday party was a big deal. A few years later we pulled out the video from the party and watched it together.

The camera was focused on my nephew as he opened presents, but in the background, you could hear my sister saying, over and over again, "What do you say, McCrae? Can you say 'thank you'? Say 'thank you!'"

McCrae was one year old at this time, sitting in a high chair with cake all over his face, and blabbering. It's doubtful whether anyone heard a "tank yu!" out of him; but over and over, you can hear Mary Brooke in the background: "What do you say, McCrae? Can you say 'thank you'?"

I love to tease Mary Brooke about this, but what she was doing was for a good reason. Why? Because gratitude is not a natural behavior—it's a learned behavior.

Why do parents have to teach their children to say "thank you"? Because children are not born all-knowing. If you've ever spent any time around babies, you begin to pick up their language. It all sounds like crying and babbling, but what they are actually saying is: "Feed me, change me, hold me, burp me, feed me some more, change me again." Everything they are saying is self-focused. Everything is all about them, all about meeting their needs. It's important that parents are intentional in teaching children the basic skills they need to be good adults. Most parents want this for their children and work with them, modeling in word and deed, how to live their lives. As children learn to practice those important life skills, those skills then become a more natural part of who they are. When they move away from home, parents pray that the children will continue to practice those habits, which we believe will serve them well in the world.

Similarly, the Apostle Paul wanted to offer training to Christians who were new in their faith. First Thessalonians is quite possibly one of the earliest documents produced in what we know as the New Testament, and in this letter, Paul is encouraging these followers of Jesus to do spiritual training. That is, to practice living their faith in action until the Lord returns. He challenges them to live a life that is pleasing to God. In doing so, he makes one of the clearest statements found in Scripture regarding God's will. According to Paul, God's will for Christians is to "Rejoice always, pray without ceasing, give thanks in all circumstances" (1 Thessalonians 5:16-18). While understanding that he was addressing a certain group of people at a certain time in history, these words also speak to us across the centuries. This is what God desires for our lives. It is what our loving Parent wants us to learn in order that we may live fully. In seeking to follow the will of God for our own lives, then, we practice and train in these spiritual habits that will enhance our lives: rejoicing, praying, and giving thanks.

Rejoice Always

Paul affirms that God's will, or desire, for our lives is that we focus on rejoicing always. Paul uses similar language in Philippians 4:4: "Rejoice in the Lord always; again I will say, Rejoice." This is easy to do when life is good and everything is going your way. But what about those times when you feel you don't have a reason to rejoice? Paul is encouraging us to make joy a way of life, a habitual holy habit. It has to do with what we choose to focus on in our lives. All of us have issues and obstacles. It's so easy to find ourselves in a place where complaining about our circumstances becomes the norm. This word to rejoice always challenges us to refocus and realize that we always have reasons to rejoice.

(Clayton) A young woman recently shared that she was reluctant to attend church when she first got out of college. When we asked why, she shared that she waited tables to help pay her way through school and that all of the waiters and waitresses tried their best to get out of the Sunday lunch shift at the restaurant because of the "church people." She said that the people coming from church were rude, acted with a sense of entitlement, and were poor tippers. Everyone hearing this story let out a collective, "Ouch!" This was her image of what Christians were like, and she wanted no part of it. Thank God she found out that not all Christians act that way, but her experience may be more the norm than not. In our society, Christians are known more for their judgment than their joy.

How will the world know the joy of living in Christ if all they see is judgment coming from Christians?

God's gift of Jesus Christ makes every day a day to rejoice. In Christ, we have been offered grace. We have been forgiven. His resurrection gives us hope in every situation. We Christians should be the most joyful people on earth. Instead, far too many of us mope around, going through the motions of life, conforming way too easily to the grumbling and grousing that marks much of our society.

(Clayton) Recently I had just had one of "those days." It started early and was one of those non-stop days going from one appointment to the next. I was not thinking about rejoicing; I was just existing, going from one thing to another. I had rushed over to a hospital to see a church member and was rushing back for a meeting. I was running late and the traffic was horrible. I pulled up at an intersection at a red light, and in the car next to me was a Labrador retriever with his head stuck out of the window. His tongue was hanging out, and it seemed that he had the biggest smile on his face, rejoicing in this wild ride called life. He looked over at me and our eyes met. This is when we had an imaginary conversation that went something like this:

Dog: "Isn't this awesome!"

Me: "What are you talking about? I'm late for a meeting. This traffic stinks. It's been a stressful day. I'm tired."

Dog: "You're missing it, man! Life is awesome! I get to ride in a car with my head out the window! My owner loves me! Life is great, and here you are moping around. You need to start enjoying life!"

When the light turned green, off went the dog with his head out the window, rejoicing in the day the Lord had made. So what did I do? I rolled down my window and stuck my head (and tongue) out and enjoyed the ride. The dog was right. Life is awesome when we take time to find joy in the everyday.

We've been challenged to make joy a way of life. It may not be a natural behavior for us, but it can be a learned behavior. We must strive every day toward this goal. It's God's will for us to live a more joy-filled life. How can you focus on finding more joy in your everyday life? How can you help others experience a more joyful life? Especially in difficult circumstances, in our own lives, in the lives of others, and in the world, we are called to be those people who are finding reasons to rejoice. Because of what God has done for us in the life, death, and resurrection of Jesus, we can learn to rejoice always.

Pray Without Ceasing

What images come to mind when you read that we are supposed to pray without ceasing? What's a realistic way to pray without ceasing? We can't sit home or go to church and pray all day. We have to go to work and do other daily chores all day long. Yet we are told God's will for us is to pray without ceasing. What does Paul mean by this?

(Clayton) I was once in a small group with an older gentleman who was very wise and deeply committed to his faith. Several of us in the group noticed that when he prayed he never said "amen" at the end of his prayers. One day one of the members asked him about it. He shared, "For most people, when they say 'amen' it's like they are hanging up the phone. 'I'm finished telling God what I needed to say. I'll call back if I need anything else.' The Bible says to pray without ceasing, and I want to keep the phone lines open. I don't say 'amen' because I'm not finished praying. I'm trying to constantly be aware of an ongoing conversation I'm having with God. The Lord may have more to say to me and I need to be listening."

Especially in difficult circumstances, in our own lives, in the lives of others, and in the world, we are called to be those people who are finding reasons to rejoice.

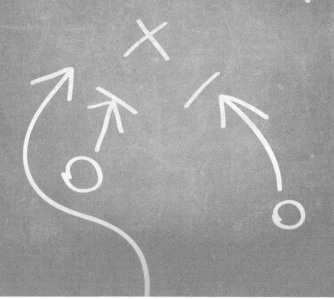

His explanation helped me understand prayer as a way of living. It is an ongoing conversation with God. Praying without ceasing is being aware of God's presence throughout the day and seeking to listen to what God is saying to us all day long.

When we make prayer a way of life, we are training ourselves in another holy habit. We grow ever more aware of God's presence in our lives. Throughout the day we are lifting up concerns, both for family and friends and the issues they are facing, as well as the concerns of the world around us. What if you began every day with a short prayer, "Lord, the lines are open and I'm listening for your voice today? Help me to hear you, to see you, and to be aware of your presence." When we make this a daily habit, we are in a training process of practicing the presence of God.

Praying may not be a natural behavior, but it can be a learned behavior. In practicing it, we may discover how God is speaking to us through situations we encounter and through people we interact with daily. Praying without ceasing isn't just about bowing our heads. It is about an ongoing conversation with the One who created us. God only desires the best for us and the world. Training ourselves to seek God, worship God, be aware of God, and call on God for help, reminds us that we have a relationship with the Source of strength, hope, and love.

What would happen in your life if you could focus on your relationship with God throughout the day? Would you find more joy? Would you be more aware of the needs of others? Would it make you more grateful for your blessings?

Give Thanks in All Circumstances

Paul's last counsel, in terms of seeking to follow God's will, is to give thanks in all circumstances. This is really challenging to do, especially when you find yourself in less-than-ideal circumstances. How are you supposed to have a spirit of gratitude when your life is falling apart? It may be helpful to note that Paul did not say, "Give thanks *for* all circumstances," but rather "*in* all circumstances." As Christians we are learning to be thankful for the blessings we have in the midst of all of life—in good times and bad times. Because of what God has done for us through the life, death, and resurrection of Jesus, there is always a reason to be grateful.

Luke 17:11-19 tells us about ten lepers Jesus encounters while going through an area on the border of Samaria and Judah. Now a good religious rabbi, or teacher of the Law, would not have gone near Samaria (because the Jews and Samaritans despised one another), but Jesus did. Jesus didn't seem to be bothered by visiting people and places that were shunned by others. From a distance, a group of ten lepers call out to him. They were careful to keep their distance, because according to the Law, a diagnosis of leprosy meant you were an outcast. People with leprosy were isolated and ostracized. Even if you just had a bad skin rash, the priest might see you and say, "You know, you might have leprosy...out to the leper's colony! You are no longer welcome in the house of the Lord. You are no longer welcome in your family group. You're no longer welcome in this town. You need to get out."

Leprosy was a death sentence. Leprosy was like being told, "You are alive, but you're no longer really here. You really don't exist anymore." Lepers were people without hope. But these ten lepers recognize Jesus and call out, "Have mercy on us!" Jesus saw their plight and gave them a command. He simply said, "Go and show yourselves to the priest." Why did Jesus tell them that? Because only the priest could restore lepers to the community. For an outcast who has been suddenly restored to his or her family and community, a healing from leprosy was like resurrection from the dead.

The story tells us they stepped out in faith. They obeyed and were healed, all ten of them. But did all ten of them run back to Jesus, fall down on their knees, and begin praising God? Did all ten say, "Thank you, Lord! Thank you, Lord, for the gift of healing! You have restored our lives; we have been resurrected and renewed! We have been given new hope and new life. Thank you, Lord"?

No! That's not what happened. Only one leper, when he saw that he was healed, turned back, praising God with a loud voice. He fell at Jesus' feet and gave thanks. He was a Samaritan, a foreigner. The one who was least likely to praise Jesus was the only one to stop and say thank you. Jesus said, "Were not ten made clean? But the other nine, where are they?"

This is an incredible, but troubling, story because it's our story. We sometimes get so caught up in our lives that we fail to stop and say thank you. Here's an important question for us: are we more like the one leper who returned to Jesus and thanked him, or more like the nine lepers who went on their way to live their lives?

The nine were probably very grateful. When they saw they were healed, they certainly wanted to see the priest as quickly as possible so they might be restored to their families, communities, and synagogues. We can imagine they ran, having good places to go, good people to see, connections to make. We know how it is, being busy doing lots of other things. They appreciated Jesus, but they didn't go back to tell him so.

Does your life look more like the nine or more like the one? Scripture teaches us something important about the Christian life: it's not just about following a set of rules, although as Christians we don't dismiss God's teachings. The Christian life should be a response of gratitude, returning daily to the Source of blessing to express gratitude. What would your life look like if you got serious about living a life of gratitude?

(Mary Brooke) I have long admired my mother-in-law, Dede, for many reasons, but especially for her "gratitude attitude." She has spoken and written on the subject, noting that gratefulness is valued by all of the world's religions, a virtue that is extolled and held in common by people of diverse cultures and faiths. She once gave each of her six grandsons a journal and encouraged them to write down five things they were grateful for every day. Her conversations are filled with expressions of gratitude about all manner of people, things and situations, great and small.

I wonder what our lives would be like if we kept a daily gratitude journal, noting five things we are grateful for. What would our lives be like if we could cultivate a "gratitude attitude"? And what difference could we make in the lives of others if our "gratitude attitude" became contagious?

Practical Training

Gratitude is not a natural behavior; it is a learned behavior. That's why as parents we teach our kids to say thank you. Are there practical ways we can train ourselves to be more grateful? Wouldn't that training make a tremendous difference in our lives—not to mention that gratitude is part of God's desire for our lives?

(Clayton) Several years ago, in a program we adapted from another church, our church spent a year focused on gratitude. We challenged our members to write personal thank-you notes, e-mails, and text messages to people for whom they were grateful. It became a contagious movement that had a powerful, spiritual impact on the life of our congregation. Making gratitude a holy habit not only changes us; it changes the people in the world around us.

There are many people we appreciate in our hearts and minds. But have we expressed our thanks and appreciation? Have we told them so? What if we were intentional in expressing gratitude on an ongoing basis to our family, our friends, those we interact with daily, strangers we meet along the way, and especially to God?

When was the last time you took a family member or friend by the hand and said, "You are such a blessing in my life. I don't tell you this enough, but I'm so grateful that God brought you into my life."

If you are a parent, it doesn't matter if your child is three years old, thirteen years old, twenty-three years old, or fifty-three years old, they can never hear from you enough, "I am so grateful you are my child." What a powerful statement it would be if you took the time to write a note of gratitude to your child. Likewise, regardless of your age, your parents would be ecstatic if they got a note from you. Can you imagine how touched they would be to receive a note from you that said, "I'm so grateful to have you as parents because…"?

What other family members would appreciate a note of gratitude? What about friends you've shared the special moments of your life with? Have you told them how much their friendship means to you? How grateful to God you are for their friendship? How would your work environment change if your coworkers knew how grateful you were for the opportunity to work beside them and you expressed it with a handwritten note? This is a contagious movement, and it might be life-changing to the people around you!

What about the people who serve us every day—sales clerks, cashiers, wait staff, and so forth. Too often, these people are "invisible" to us. How might they feel about their jobs and themselves if we expressed our gratitude for their service?

(Clayton) I heard a story of a church member who went out of his home to greet the workers from the trash pickup service as they made their weekly rounds. He gave each one a cold bottle of water, saying, "I'm so grateful for you and your work." It's easy to say of those who serve us, "Well, that's their job; they get paid to do that." But in a Christlike manner, I'm inspired by this man's offering of a cold drink and a blessing.

Ninety percent of those healed from the leper colony that Jesus passed through went on about their lives as if their healing were simply good fortune. They may have been grateful, but they didn't express it. Only one out of ten went back to express gratitude.

So, again, we must ask ourselves, are we more like the one leper who returned to Jesus and thanked him, or more like the nine lepers who went on their way? Does my life look more like the one or more like the nine? Every day brings a new opportunity to decide!

Grateful to God

What does gratitude look like when it comes to our relationship with God? Are there days when we're so busy we forget to give thanks to God? It's probably not that we aren't grateful, but like the nine lepers, we don't always express our thanks. We fail to acknowledge God as the Giver of all good gifts—the One who has forgiven our sins and restored us to life, the One who gives us hope when we feel like all hope has been cut off.

Perhaps that's why Jesus noticed that only one leper returned to give thanks. Jesus knew that gratitude is a key component of a healthy relationship. In some sense, we are all lepers, and ingratitude is leprosy of the soul. It eventually eats away at our relationships and robs our quality of life.

Jesus seemed disappointed and surprised that nine of the ten did not express gratitude to him for their healing. And yet, Jesus was grateful for the one leper who came back to give thanks and praise. And it seems that the one leper got a double blessing, with Jesus saying to him alone, "Get up and go your way; your faith has made you well." *Wellness* is the same word for *wholeness*. While all the lepers were healed, this one was made whole. He completed the healing when he expressed his gratitude to the Healer.

Expressing gratitude to God is an expression of faith in God. It's our way of acknowledging God as the Giver of Life, the Giver of all that we have and are.

(Mary Brooke) I always knew when our parents were awake in the morning, because I would hear them loudly proclaim: "This is the day that the Lord has made; / let us rejoice and be glad in it" (Psalm 118:24). Praising God every morning for the gift of a new day helps set a tone of gratitude to God throughout the day.

We need to remember that before we can go forward to address our many daily responsibilities, we need to "go back" to God and say "thanks." We need to acknowledge our gratitude toward God, from whom all blessings flow, the Source and Center of our lives. And in doing so, like the one leper, we may find a double blessing!

Like an athlete training to improve in her or his sport, we have to be intentional in training for life. Rejoicing, praying, and giving thanks may not be the most natural behaviors for us, but through perpetual practice, we can learn how to do them. When we do so, they become a more natural expression of our lives, and life is more blessed because it is more aligned with God's will and desire for our lives. As the great football coach Vince Lombardi once said to his team, "Perfection is not attainable. But if we chase perfection, we can catch excellence."[1]

Praising God every morning for the gift of a new day helps set a tone of gratitude to God throughout the day.

How much more excellent would life be—in our homes, in our schools, in our churches, and in our communities—if all followers of Christ relentlessly pursued living into God's will by rejoicing always, praying without ceasing, and giving thanks in all circumstances? If you want to get in the game, you have to do some training. Rejoicing, praying, and giving thanks are good places to start.

This is the day the Lord has made! I will rejoice and be glad in it! And through this day, Lord, help me to be less judgmental and more joyful. I open myself to be in conversation with you throughout this day. Help me to experience your presence. Open my eyes and ears, that I may see you, hear you, and worship you throughout this day. And Lord, most of all this day, I want to say thank you. Thank you for sending Jesus to be my Savior. Thank you for the many blessings you have poured into my life. Forgive me for those times I have been blessed by you, but like the nine healed lepers, I walked away. Help me always to be grateful in all circumstances, for you are my God, my Guide, and my Friend. So be it. And Lord, I will keep the line open all day, listening for you. In Jesus' name. Amen.

REFLECT

X A Disciple's Playbook

Reread 1 Thessalonians 5:16-18 and Luke 17:11-19 (see page 64).

First Thessalonians may be the earliest document in the New Testament. Paul is writing to those who have responded to the gospel message. Some of these believers evidently faced open hostility from those who rejected this message, as we read in 1 Thessalonians 1:6, "And you became imitators of us and of the Lord, for in spite of persecution you received the word with joy inspired by the Holy Spirit." In 1 Thessalonians 5:16-18, Paul directly appeals to God's will in terms of their proper behavior.

They are first called to "rejoice always." This closely mirrors Paul's encouragement to the church at Philippi, "Rejoice in the Lord, always; again I will say, Rejoice" (Philippians 4:4). Christians can rejoice always because of what God has done for us in the life, death, and resurrection of Jesus. Our situation may not be joyful, but God is a source of joy in all situations.

Paul also admonishes the believers to "pray without ceasing." Paul and his friends have indeed been doing this very thing for the Thessalonian believers, as he says in 1 Thessalonians 3:10: "Night and day we pray most earnestly that we may see you face to face and restore whatever is lacking in your faith." This is a word of encouragement to stay connected to God through every circumstance we face in life.

"Give thanks in all circumstances" completes these three sayings that Paul says are "the will of God in Christ Jesus for you." Being grateful is easy when all is well. Paul's challenge is to find gratitude in your heart, no matter what has happened. Again, because of what God has done for us in Jesus, we always have a reason to be grateful. Practicing gratitude is a spiritual discipline that opens us to understand God's desire for our lives. When we learn this behavior, it changes our lives, giving us a different perspective no matter what we are going through.

Luke's telling of Jesus and the ten lepers is a story unique to Luke's Gospel. Lepers were outcasts and could not come within a certain distance of healthy people. It had to do with both fear of the disease spreading and the cleansing rituals of being pure before God in order to be a part of the community. Lepers often had to beg for food, appealing to the compassion of strangers. Jesus is moved by their plight, has mercy upon them, and offers healing. As they go to show themselves to the priests, a step required to verify their health status, they all realize they have been healed. One stops to go back. Luke tells us he is a Samaritan. Jesus also lifts up a Samaritan as a positive role model in Luke 10:28-37. The Samaritans and Jews despised each other, a feud going back centuries, after the return from the Exile. That Luke uses another Samaritan in a positive light reminds us of the inclusive nature of God's love. Jesus came for all, not just the Hebrew people, but for the whole world. The invitation is for all.

Jesus says that the man who showed gratitude is made whole, another word for *salvation*. While the others are healed, there is a qualitative difference for the man who showed gratitude. Gratitude has that impact upon our lives. Many of us go through our lives and have amazing blessings. But how often do we truly stop and express gratitude for those blessings? Jesus lifts up the foreigner as the one who got it right. Living gratefully is a lifestyle, and one that takes practice.

How can you train yourself to rejoice, pray, and give thanks in all circumstances?

Does your life look more like the one or more like the nine?

◎ Game Plan

What insights did you gain from each section of this chapter?

Rejoice Always

Pray Without Ceasing

Give Thanks in All Circumstances

Practical Training

Grateful to God

 Score

What's the "winning point" you will remember from this chapter?

CHAPTER 4

ALL IN

A Life of Generosity

We want you to know, brothers and sisters, about the grace of God that has been granted to the churches of Macedonia; for during a severe ordeal of affliction, their abundant joy and their extreme poverty have overflowed in a wealth of generosity on their part. For, as I can testify, they voluntarily gave according to their means, and even beyond their means, begging us earnestly for the privilege of sharing in this ministry to the saints—and this, not merely as we expected; they gave themselves first to the Lord and, by the will of God, to us, so that we might urge Titus that, as he had already made a beginning, so he should also complete this generous undertaking among you. Now as you excel in everything—in faith, in speech, in knowledge, in utmost eagerness, and in our love for you—so we want you to excel also in this generous undertaking.... Each of you must give as you have made up your mind, not reluctantly or under compulsion, for God loves a cheerful giver.

(2 Corinthians 8:1-7; 9:7)

CHAPTER 4

ALL IN

A Life of Generosity

When an athlete plays a sport, she or he has an important decision to make. In a sense each has to ask, "How much of myself am I going to give to this effort?" After all, playing a sport is challenging. It requires lots of practice, eating healthy, and continually striving to get better. It's not just about the glory of the game; it's also about the daily commitment. This involves the mental aspect of the game. It's the challenge to be fully committed to the cause. When you get off the sidelines and get into the game, the coach wants to know that you are "all in."

(Clayton) I've had the same experience twice in my life—once while I was in Central America and again in Africa. Both times I was attending worship services in communities that made me realize anew how wealthy we are living in a first-world country. Even those of us who don't feel particularly wealthy in comparison to others are wealthier than the majority of people in the world. And in the communities where these worship experiences took place, I was very aware of my material wealth.

A strange thing happened in both of those worship experiences—when it came time for the offering, the people began to rejoice! They broke out in applause, and they began to celebrate. There was music, and drums, and a big raucous celebration as people were exclaiming: "It's time for the offering!" The first time this happened, I turned to the pastor after the service and asked, "Is there a big celebration like that every week when the offering is taken?" He said, "You don't understand. They are so grateful that they have the opportunity to give anything. They are so grateful to be able to participate in the offering that they can't help but rejoice."

It was a powerful lesson to me in what it means to be fully committed to Christ. These people were all in with their prayers, their presence, their service, their witness, and their gifts.

What's your response when you hear, "It's time for the offering"? Are you excited about the opportunity to give, or are you a begrudging giver?

The "Want To" Spirit

Paul wrote to the church at Corinth about the churches in Macedonia. Corinth was a center of commerce, a major trade center—people were moving there, and property values were therefore probably increasing. Perhaps they had excellent schools, nice restaurants, and stores, not unlike many fast-growing metropolitan areas of our day. They were building and thriving. Compared to the wealth we see in the world today, the church at Corinth would not have been considered rich. But compared to the churches in Macedonia, they had so much more. The churches in Macedonia were struggling with basic needs. They had so little to give. In fact, they were so poverty-stricken that when Paul went there, he made a decision. He was not going to ask them to participate in the mission relief offering he was taking.

What was the "relief offering"? Everywhere in Paul's letters, as you follow his travels in the New Testament, he was taking up a relief offering for the saints at the Jerusalem church. This is first mentioned by the writer (Luke) of Acts 11:27-30. The Jerusalem church was the mother church, and it had fallen on hard times. So as Paul preached at different churches and synagogues, going about on his missionary journeys, he would ask them to give a love offering—a relief offering—for the saints at Jerusalem. Because of their own extreme poverty, Paul wasn't even going to ask the churches at Macedonia to participate in the relief offering, but the people came to him and surprised him by begging for the opportunity to give. They had heard about the relief offering, and wanted to be a part of it.

The people of Macedonia lived in extreme poverty, but they had a desire to give. Paul uses this occasion to challenge the Corinthian church, which had far more resources, by telling them about this astounding experience he had among the churches of Macedonia. He asked the Corinthians to look inside their hearts. Were they willing not only to give, but to have the same spirit about it as the Macedonians did? Could he count on the Corinthians to be "all in," like the Macedonians?

This story challenges all of us to look in our own hearts and souls when it comes to how we handle our resources, and more important, our spirit of generosity. The Macedonians exhibit some qualities we would do well to imitate. First of all, this passage speaks to their desire to give. The people of Macedonia had a "want to" spirit about giving. Have you ever seen people who have a "want to" attitude about things? Watching any given game in sports, sometimes it's obvious one team is more talented than another team. There are certain things that can't be coached in terms of talent and skills, but sometimes you see a team that has the "want to." They might be the most talented team or they might *not* be the most talented team, but what they have is heart and will and desire. There's a special joy in watching teams like that play, particularly the "underdog" teams. They have the kind of heart and soul that says: "We are not going to lose. You may beat us on the scoreboard, but the scoreboard is not what we are interested in. We are not going to lose. We are all in." They have the "want to."

(Clayton) I know a couple who define for me what "want to" looks like. Several years ago our church made the decision to relocate to a larger piece of property, less than a mile from where we were located. The church conducted a capital campaign to purchase the land, and the congregation made pledges toward that purchase.

This highly committed couple, who were active in teaching and leading Bible studies, made a decision that they would live on one of their salaries and donate the other's salary toward the new land. For me, their commitment symbolized the "want to" the congregation had in order to accomplish the goal of reaching more people and blessing our community.

After the land was paid for, we raised the funds for the first phase of our new facility. When this couple came to me and told me they had become accustomed to living on one salary and had decided to again donate the other salary for another three-year period, I nearly fainted. For six years they lived on one salary and gave the other salary to their church. They were "all in"! Of course, I'm keenly aware that many do not have the financial "margin" to be able to donate an entire salary, and I'm not suggesting that is the benchmark for being "all in." But regardless of our income level, we can be equally committed to giving generously of what we have been given.

Have you ever felt God challenge you to expand your reach, to be a part of something bigger than yourself? Something that will bless others? Something that will truly reflect the world God imagines?

It's important to understand and remember that it's not about the amount; it's about the "want to." That's what Paul saw in the churches of Macedonia, and he wanted to relay that to the Corinthian church. The Corinthian church had ability and wealth and all kinds of opportunities that the Macedonian churches didn't have. But if the Macedonian churches could do it, the Corinthian church could do it too.

Generosity and Gratitude

Another aspect 2 Corinthians 8 speaks to is the generosity and gratitude of the Macedonians. They not only had the desire, or the "want to," they also had grateful and generous hearts. There is a great phrase in the passage that says: "Their extreme poverty [has] overflowed in a wealth of generosity on their part" (v. 2). Out of the extreme poverty, it overflowed: they rejoiced and gave generously. It makes no sense. If it read "out of their extreme abundance, they gave generously," that's one thing. But the people Paul is talking about had nothing to give—but they wanted to participate.

Why? Because they recognized that God had been so good to them in giving them the gift of Jesus Christ. Out of the joy of that experience of God's grace, their lives overflowed. It was not just about their gifts; it was about everything in their beings that overflowed in this generosity. Have you ever noticed the connection between generosity and gratitude? Have you wondered which begets the other? Are people grateful because they are generous, or are they generous because they are grateful?

Perhaps people who are grateful for what they have and focus not on the blessing of riches but on the richness of blessings, are more generous people and live more generous lives, not only with finances, but with everything that they are. That includes their time and talent and ability.

(Clayton) Several years ago I officiated at the wedding of Cincinnati Bengal quarterback Andy Dalton, and his wife, Jordan, who grew up in our church. It has been incredible to see what they have done with what they have been given. Many professional athletes focus on what they can get with their newfound money and fame. Andy and Jordan started a foundation dedicated to providing seriously ill and physically challenged children with daily support and life-changing experiences. They are using their time, talent, and treasure to make a difference in the lives of others.

There is something about people who are set free by an experience of gratitude—it gives them the ability to enter into life fully. And we all have that ability through the gift of God's Son, Jesus Christ.

(**Clayton**) When I was sixteen, I had a life-shaping experience. Late one night, as our mother was paying bills at our kitchen table, I snuck up behind her with the intent of scaring her. But as I glanced over her shoulder at the check she was writing, I was the one who was shocked. I said, "Mother, what are you doing? Do you give that much to the church every month?"

To me, the amount she was writing on the check seemed far out of proportion to our income. Our father was a pastor, and my mother had taken a part-time job to help supplement our income. I had a rough idea of what the family income was, and, at sixteen, I was thinking only about myself—the idea of a car was in my mind. Yet here were my parents giving away this money.

She asked me to sit down, and asked, "How many meals did you eat today?" I lamely responded, "Three," although at that age I had probably eaten more than that. She continued, "We have a home to live in, clothes to wear, and everything we need." She explained that she and my father had made a decision to be a tithing family years before, giving 10 percent of their income to the work of God, and the first check they wrote each month was to the church. The amount she had written to the church was actually the amount they gave every two weeks. She concluded her speech to me by saying, "God has been so good to us, and we are so grateful. This is one of the ways we can express our gratitude."

It was one of the moments in my youth when I really understood who my parents were and what they were all about. Their example informed the decision my wife and I made to be a tithing family as well. I always stood in awe of their generosity, not just in terms of finances, but in every area of their lives.

Years later, after both of my parents had died, in going through the settlement of their estate, we discovered that they had been giving around 20 percent of their income to the work of God through their church and other mission work. They gave because they were so grateful to God.

One way to think about faith is that it is a grateful response to the gift God has given us through Jesus, and this response encompasses our whole lives. It's not just the giving of our financial support; it also includes all that we have and all that we are. When we focus on the richness of our blessings, something happens to our perspective. Our wealth is measured not by the amount in our bank accounts, but by the many blessings God has given to us. Too often people confuse their net worth and their self-worth. If we focused on how good God has been to us in giving us Jesus, in opening up life and all of its possibilities to us, many more of us would feel rich. We have all been blessed, most of all by God's love for us through Christ.

There is something
about people who
are set free by an
experience of gratitude—
it gives them the ability
to enter into life fully.

(Mary Brooke) Our dad loved to tell a story from his pastor days. He was trying to raise money for a new youth center at the church he served, and he and a layman chairing the project went to visit a man who had been very financially successful in his business. The man and his wife had four children who were active in the youth program.

After telling the man about the vision the church had for reaching and serving youth and showing him the plans for the new center, our dad and the layman asked the man for a pledge to the capital campaign. The man told them he was not able to make a contribution. They thanked him for his time and left.

The man's daughter asked her father why their pastor and a lay leader of the church had come to call on him. He told her the reason for their visit.

"So, how much did you give to the new youth center?" she asked.

"Well, I told them we were not able to make a gift," he told her.

The young girl gave her dad an incredulous look and waved her hand around their spacious, lovely residence. "Dad, if *we* can't give something, then who can?" she asked.

The following morning, after a sleepless night, the man called our dad and told him about the conversation with his daughter. He said he and his family would be making a sizable contribution to the new youth center.

Our family has remembered that story often over the years. We've seen people in extreme poverty, like the Macedonians, give generously and joyously. We've seen people of extreme wealth, like the Corinthians, give generously and joyously. And we've remembered those prophetic words from a young girl who gratefully acknowledged her family's blessings: "If *we* can't give something, then who can?"

Giving Ourselves to the Lord

Paul lifts up another aspect of the remarkable Macedonian response when he says, "They gave themselves first to the Lord" (2 Corinthians 8:5). That was their motive for everything else they did. Paul is letting us know they had their priorities straight—put God first and everything else falls into place. While that can sound like a cliché, many followers of Jesus have found this to be a formula that makes life work best. Some people try to fit God into their lives, as if God, or their relationship to the church, is just one activity among many. Church often gets squeezed out of the equation due to select sports, weekend activities, or a desire to sleep in. But when God becomes the priority, the other things in life tend to take their place in a way that makes more sense. Some things fall by the wayside because we realize that, in the long run, they are not as important. Other things, still very important to us, tend to find their rightful place. They are important, but not priority. We give ourselves first to the Lord.

In his book *Essentialism: The Disciplined Pursuit of Less*, author Greg McKeown points out that the word *priority* first appears in the English language in the 1400s. It was singular for the next five hundred years. Only in the 1900s did we start talking about "priorities."[1]

"If *we* can't give something, then who can?"

McKeown suggests that somehow we think we can bend reality—that is, by pluralizing the word, we can somehow have multiple things that we call "first" in our lives.[2] This is a sin many of us find ourselves guilty of, and as a result, we end up trying to be all things to all people. The truth is, we can't have multiple priorities. There cannot be three or six things at the top of our list, and our lives still make sense. We must choose, like Joshua, who said, "As for me and my household, we will serve the LORD" (Joshua 24:15). The Apostle Paul is so impressed by the way the Macedonian Christians have made Christ the priority of their lives that he lifts it up to the Corinthian Christians as a true example of the way followers of Jesus should live.

(Mary Brooke) My first job as a college graduate was with a communications office that produced publications for church institutions. This gave me an opportunity to interview donors who gave generously to various ministries, such as children's homes and retirement homes. For the first time, I realized the privilege wealth afforded in being able to give significant gifts that would make a difference in many lives. I also was impressed by persons who lived frugally, leaving their life savings to bless and benefit others. But more than anything, I came to understand the joy of responding to God's love and goodness generously.

As I heard the stories of people who gave to these particular ministries, I was touched by their laser focus on Christ as their motivation. The lesson I learned was that the amount we give is not as important as the reason we give. This prompted me to pray about my own giving habits. From this period of discernment emerged these words: "Because I'm forgiven, I'm for giving."

To this day, as I recall Christ's death on the cross for our sins, his grace and forgiveness, his invitation to new life, I realize that my gifts are a small but important way of expressing my gratitude to the One who gave his all.

Cheerful Giving

One last thing that Paul shares in lifting up the example of the Macedonian Christians is important: no one should give under compulsion. Giving, whether we are talking about our financial resources, our service to others, or whatever other gifts we have to offer, should be given cheerfully and freely. Just as the Macedonians had rejoiced over the opportunity to be a part of the relief offering for the saints in Jerusalem, so Paul was encouraging the Corinthians to give out of gladness, not out of guilt.

Too many Christians (and non-Christians) have had bad experiences with churches and money. No one should ever feel forced to give. The guilt trips that some pastors and lay leaders use to raise money for different causes does not encourage long-term development of Christian stewards. Rather, it turns people away from wanting to be a part of a church community. Manipulating people is a poor substitute for having a compelling vision that beckons people to participate in it. What a difference it makes when people give out of a sense of joy.

(Clayton) When I served as pastor of another church, I would often stop at a nearby donut shop on my way to the church. The woman who owned the shop was a member of a Korean church in our community. I had preached there and she knew I was a pastor. She always had the most cheerful smile for her customers. Whenever I came in, she would not allow me to pay. She would insist, "You don't pay, you pray." After a while I began to feel guilty about her giving me free donuts, so I started leaving money beside the cash register when she turned to put my donuts in a bag.

I thought I was doing a good thing, but one day her pastor called and asked if he could come see me. He explained that the woman was very distraught that I was leaving money. What she was doing for me, she was doing cheerfully. It gave her joy to bless another person, especially a pastor. It was something she wanted to do for me. The pastor's words really stung when he said, "You are robbing her of her joy in giving." It was then that I understood what Paul meant by cheerfully giving, as well as cheerfully receiving.

Our giving to God should come out of our glad and generous hearts. God has been so good to us—that is why we give. We give to causes we believe in, causes where we see something compelling happening. We don't *have* to give to those causes, we *want* to! We see in those organizations a sense of purpose, that they are truly making a difference, and not just paying the bills. When we find those causes, we have a joy about giving, knowing we are helping to make a difference.

All In

There is something about a people who honor God first and foremost with their lives. What if we committed to "give ourselves first to the Lord"? What if we began to imagine what God imagines for our world, our homes, our church, and for us individually? What if we proclaimed, "God has blessed us, each one of us! Every one of us has something to offer, to the world, to the church, to God"? And what if, when it's time to offer our gifts to God, there overflowed extreme generosity and rejoicing, out of our abundance—or out of poverty—in whatever situation we find ourselves in today, because we first gave ourselves to the Lord? Can you imagine that, instead of murmuring or moaning when it came time to collect the offering at your church, people suddenly started celebrating and rejoicing for the opportunity to be a part of something special?

When it comes to our faith in Christ, God has called us to be "all in." What if we sang the hymn, "I Surrender All" and we meant it? Not "I surrender some," but "I surrender all." Truthfully, there are times when the thought of giving our lives, and everything we are, to Christ is a little overwhelming. But God has an amazing vision for our lives. Working with God, focusing on the basics, getting in the zone, training daily to follow God's will, and giving our lives—all in—to God, we can step closer toward that vision.

May God give us the "want to" as we walk forward in faith. May we get in the game rather than sit on the sidelines. May we serve God cheerfully all of our days.

Dear God, what a gift you have given to us. Yet so often I focus on what I don't have, instead of what I do have. Teach me that I am rich, regardless of my material possessions. I am rich because you have given Jesus to the world and to me. This day, O Lord, in response to this amazing gift, I give myself fully to you. You are my one true priority. I will serve you with joy and gladness. Use me as you will and where you will. I am all in for you. In whatever ways I can, use my gifts to bless others in this world. In Jesus' name I pray. Amen.

REFLECT

⟩A Disciple's Playbook

Reread 2 Corinthians 8:1-7; 9:7 (see page 88).

One of the aspects of Paul's missionary journeys, recorded in the Book of Acts and revealed in some of his letters, is the relief offering for the saints in the mother church in Judea. The offering is first mentioned in Acts 11:27-30 and is referenced in Romans 15:26, among other places. The extreme poverty that Paul finds when he arrives in Macedonia makes him conclude that he will not ask these believers to be a part of this offering. However, perhaps because of their own experience of God's provision and grace, they have an "abundance of joy" that overflows into a "wealth of generosity." They may not have been able to give much, but they were overjoyed to offer what they could. They lived their faith as a response of gratitude for what God had done for them.

What would it mean for you to give yourself first to the Lord?

How can you be more generous with your time, talents, and treasure?

◎ Game Plan

What insights did you gain from each section of this chapter?

The "Want To" Spirit

Generosity and Gratitude

Giving Ourselves to the Lord

Cheerful Giving

All In

 Score

What's the "winning point" you will remember from this chapter?

NOTES

Chapter 1: Focus on the Basics

1. Adam Hamilton, *The Way: 40 Days of Reflection: Walking in the Footsteps of Jesus* (Nashville, TN: Abingdon Press, 2013), 71.
2. Bible Hub, s.v. "Pharisaios," accessed September 19, 2015, http://biblehub.com/greek/5330.htm.
3. Mendy Hecht, "The 613 Commandments," *Chabad-Lubavitch Media Center*, accessed September 20, 2015, http://www.chabad.org/library/article_cdo /aid/756399/jewish/The-613-Commandments.htm.
4. Ibid.
5. Jewish Virtual Library, s.v. "Jewish Concepts: Mitzvot," American-Israeli Cooperative Enterprise, accessed September 23, 2015, https://www .jewishvirtuallibrary.org/jsource/Judaism /mitzvot.html.

6. See Robert Schnase, *Five Practices of Fruitful Congregations* (Nashville, TN: Abingdon Press, 2007), 59-78.

Chapter 2: Get in the Zone

1. "The Baptismal Covenant I," *The United Methodist Hymnal* (Nashville, TN: The United Methodist Publishing House, 1989), 34.

Chapter 3: Training

1. Vince Lombardi, "Famous Quotations by Vince Lombardi," *VinceLombardi.com*, accessed September 29, 2015, http://www.vincelombardi.com /quotes.html.

Chapter 4: All In: A Life of Generosity

1. Greg McKeown, *Essentialism: The Disciplined Pursuit of Less* (New York: Crown Business/Penguin Random House, 2014), 16.
2. Ibid.

ACKNOWLEDGMENTS

(Clayton) So many people have helped give shape to the formulation of this material. Writing with my sister, Mary Brooke Casad, has been and continues to be a joyous experience. She is one of the most creative, dedicated people I know; a person who truly strives to live her faith in word and deed. Many of the stories we use to illustrate the Scriptures in The Basics series come out of our family experiences in both joyful and trying times. You are a blessing!

I'm grateful to the Worship Team and staff of First United Methodist Church, Richardson, Texas, who helped develop the sermon series in which some of these messages originally appeared, and the congregation who first heard these messages and gave good feedback. Jennifer Rawlinson and Drew Presley were helpful early on in the process with sermon transcriptions. I am always thankful for the many mentors who have blessed my life, particularly my preaching mentor, Dr. Don Benton, and preaching professor, Dr. Zan W. Holmes, Jr.

My wife, Lori, and children, Erin, Katy, and Grant, continue to bring so much joy to my life. They have put up with my writing and offered gracious feedback as well as constant encouragement and support. Thank you all for blessing my life!

(Mary Brooke) I'm profoundly grateful for the opportunity to co-author The Basics series with Clayton, who besides being my biological brother is a true brother in Christ. His genuine faith is lived out authentically in every aspect of his life, bringing blessing and joy to me and to many others. Thank you, Clayton!

Our stories reflect the blessings of family, friends, and communities of faith who have enriched and shaped us. Except for our family members, the names of other persons in our stories have been changed. I give thanks to God for all who have been a part of my faith journey.

With gratitude for their support, encouragement, and love, I offer my heartfelt thanks to my husband, Vic, and our family: Carter, McCrae, Melissa, Revol, Patrick, and Ana. (And a special word of thanks to McCrae for assisting with the transcriptions of his uncle's sermons!)

We both gratefully acknowledge Neil Alexander and the wonderful folks at The United Methodist Publishing House. A special word of appreciation goes to Susan Salley and Sally Sharpe. Thank you!